MARION TANNER

START A COACHING BUSINESS ONLINE

The Ultimate Guide on How to Start an Online Coaching Business, Learn How You Can Use Your Knowledge, Talent and Expertise to Start a Successful Coaching Business

Descrierea CIP a Bibliotecii Naţionale a României
MARION TANNER
    START A COACHING BUSINESS ONLINE. The Ultimate
Guide on How to Start an Online Coaching Business, Learn How
You Can Use Your Knowledge, Talent and Expertise to Start a
Successful Coaching Business / Marion Tanner – Bucharest: Editura
My Ebook, 2021
    ISBN

MARION TANNER

START A COACHING BUSINESS ONLINE

The Ultimate Guide on How to Start an Online Coaching Business, Learn How You Can Use Your Knowledge, Talent and Expertise to Start a Successful Coaching Business

My Ebook Publishing House
Bucharest, 2021

TABLE OF CONTENTS

START AN ONLINE COACHING BUSINESS USING YOUR TALENTS AND EXPERTISE

Learning something new is fun; it can also be a challenge. Many times we are required to learn something new with our job and there are times when we are interested in something and want to learn more about it. That's why a coaching business offers a great way to make some nice profits.

There is so much information out there so it seems very easy to just do some research and find what it is you need to know. How easy is it to apply your new found knowledge in a real life situation, and how much can you trust the information out there? It is not really that simple. Learning something and doing something are two different things.

Learning something and putting it into practice takes time, patience, and a good coach. This is where you come in handy. Think of your current niche, and as you are thinking about it, is there something within your niche that people need or want help with? Maybe you cannot think of something within your niche, so below are ten coaching businesses examples.

The purpose is to give you the coacher ideas within different niches, then go back and think of ways you can create a coaching business within your own niche. If you still cannot think of anything within your niche, then it can be a totally separate business from what you have right now. Read each one and think about it. Then read it again thinking of ways you can apply that knowledge to your own business.

Types of Coaching Businesses

The ten coaching business ideas are computer/IT, financial, career, parenting, gardening, school (high school and college), cooking, instruments, hone improvement, and sales. Each one is a different type of business, and you may or may not need any special experience to start. You won't need experience to start the business either, but one thing to note is you must let your potential clients know you are simply coaching and not giving professional advice.

If you are a professional, that is great and you will be a step ahead of others coachers out there. But nonetheless, people will seek a non-professional who charges less to give supplemental knowledge to what they already know.

Another thing is do not limit your thoughts and beliefs to what is written. You are encouraged to take these types of coaching business ideas and come up with creative ways to start your own business with your skills and expertise.

Computer and IT

Computers are designed to help you to become more productive. But there are times when they can slow us down.

If you are great with computers, you can start a coaching business to help with those pesky issues that get in the way of getting your daily tasks done. Let me walk you through some ideas to get you started with this type of business.

If someone has a minor issue and he or she cannot afford to pay a professional, you can charge a lower rate and coach them through the issue from home. Maybe it's not computer issues that you can help with. There are many new computer programmers out there who may need a little coaching to help them apply what they learned in school to their career.

Financial

Money management can be very tough for many people. It is very important to have your finances in order so you are prepared for now and your future. You know the saying "save your pennies for a rainy day." You literally need to save your money so that it works for you and not against you. So many people borrow more than they make in one year.

The best way to help anyone is to help them before they get into a financial bind. You are there to help people make sound financial decisions, and coaching will greatly motivate people to take action and be wise with their money. It is heartbreaking to see people when they lose so many things they worked so hard to get. Financial coaching may be the most sought after and necessary business today.

When people get into desperate situations they look for someone to help them out. Their reasons for creating this problem are all different, but in this day and age, it is hard to survive on the little income most people make. There are however, ways to manage your money well and live off of the income you have and be in good financial standing.

So as a financial coach, you will be giving sound advice and helping people learn how money works. You may also help them grow their wealth and use certain people for your resources such as Warren Buffet, Napoleon Hill, and Dave Ramsey to name a few. These people and more helped many people make their money work for them.

Career Coaching

Your career is the most important decision you will need to make in life. It will give you income and ultimately help you to decide your best path through life. It is hard for some people to decide which career path will ultimately allow them to live the life they choose.

You might believe your dream of becoming a doctor or nurse when you were five years old is the best career choice. When you reach adulthood however, your way of thinking may change significantly. In reality, the best way to choose a career that is most fitting to you is one that reflects the lifestyle you want. There are tests you can take and studies performed that act as a guide and give you advice on a career but, may not be a definite answer.

So if you have a lot of knowledge about careers and which ones are ideal for certain personalities, then you can make a nice business reflecting what you know about it to clients. Sometimes it helps if you studied psychology because much of how you match someone up with an ideal career has a lot to do with his or her psyche.

Do remember this and all businesses in this article are ones you will not need previous experience to start, but it does require some ability to work well with others. You need to be good with people, understand their concerns, and attract people who are willing to take advice. They should be informed that the final outcome of the coaching sessions is a reflection of their choices. You are only there to help them see things with a different perspective.

Parenting

Having children is a blessing. Knowing effective ways to parent your children can seem obscure or even a little difficult at times. You will also notice each child is different. The best advice for someone to start a parenting coaching career is to have some background working with children. It is even a good idea to have a degree in child psychology, but not required.

Whichever coaching business you decide to start is designed to give people advice and supplemental knowledge. Look for people who are willing to take advice as sometimes giving parenting advice can turn people off.

When you get the chance, look up a show called "Nanny 911" and learn from it. These professionals have helped many families get their children on the right track behaviorally. If you notice, a lot of it has to do with the parent changing the ways they believe they should discipline their children. Success only comes from taking the advice the nannies give and working with their children in a consistent manner.

So if you feel you have what it takes and love working with children and are good at helping other see things from a different view, then this can be a very rewarding business choice. Remember the world needs people who are willing to help others in need.

Gardening

No matter what season it is, people love to garden. Some have indoor plants and others plant during the spring and summer months outside. Others have greenhouses where they can plant any time of the year. No matter how you setup your garden, I always hear people say they do not have a green thumb and their plants will not last.

It is those people who many times want to learn to garden but feel they do not have what it takes. This is where a gardening coach comes in handy. There are many facets and different crucial elements that go into gardening to have the most success with it. Each plant is not created equal and will require different types of attention and nutrition.

If you are great at gardening and have had much success with it, then you might consider coaching others through it. It is always best to have a coach of some sort help another person. Hearing the advice and seeing it put into action are very different. There is also terminology that is easier to show than to just know the definition.

School (High School and College)

Learning is very rewarding but can be challenging at times. It does not matter who you are, your upbringing, or how well you absorb information. As a child, many times you can absorb information like a sponge. However, when you reach adulthood, learning is NOT the same. There are many resources out there to help you learn something, but there is no such thing as too much help.

With so many learning styles and information changing so rapidly, there is a NEED for people to coach others through their learning experience. Now there will most likely be some subjects you excel at and others you are not so great at. So think about what you are good at and work with people with that subject.

Cooking

When you open your Facebook or Twitter profile, you will notice there are a lot of recipes and videos of people making the recipe. They look so good and so you just want to try it. For some reason, you quickly think, "I won't be able to make it as good as they did in the video." But you know that simply is not true.

You probably will not be making a career out of a few people who just have an interest in making one simple recipe, but rather someone who has a deeper interest in it. So how will you know if they do or not? You can look at the comments on the video to get an idea of how to market this type of coaching business, but may never know who is really interested until they respond to you ad.

To advertise your cook coaching business make your own video of a recipe and put a link in it or in the description letting people know you have coaching sessions for people who want to become chefs or improve their cooking skills.

Instruments

Music is often considered a universal language. It reaches deep down in our souls and touches many generations. When you like something you are listening to, you will put your own meaning to it. No matter what language you speak, music will be interpreted in your own language even when you do not understand the words and their meaning.

People want to carry on a legacy that has been passed down for generations, or they want to make a crowd of people have a great time. No matter what the reason, learning instruments is, and will be in high demand for a long time.

If you know an instrument and have a passion for helping others learn to play, you are on the fast track to growing a lucrative business and earning many clients.

What instruments are easy to learn without being face to face with an instructor? Pretty much every instrument on the planet and that is due to video and web cameras.

Home Improvement

Your house is your home. You want it to be more than just a building you eat, relax, and sleep in. It is a part of your well-being. Keeping your home in working order and having it look presentable is something we all desire. Sometimes we do not know where to start and we begin to look for some good advice.

If you have the expertise in home improvement, then why not create a coaching program for it? For example, say you want to lay new tile in your kitchen. It may seem like no brainer, but there are actually some important things to keep in mind so you can prepare yourself before you start. The measurements of course along with how to prepare the sub-floor and so on are all things a good coach can help with.

Sales

Selling is a part of life. Whether you realize it or not, when you go to a job interview, you are "selling" your expertise and skills to the potential employer. People think of sales in a negative connotation, but here is your chance to show people that it is not so bad. Plus people who are already in the sales profession know that they always need to find ways to improve.

This is why sales coaching will be a great profit maker for you. More and more people are starting their own businesses, and guess what; sales are going to and always will be a big part of it. How else will you get your clients? Selling is a must, but unlike the old days, the strategies used to sell have changed dramatically.

For this section, I will talk about different selling styles. First selling is not something that can be forced upon others. Whatever way you word things, a "NO" most likely will be a

NO. You have to respect that no and realize you do not want to do business with someone who gives you a negative response.

What are some selling styles? Proactive, consultative, aggressive, and passive are some of the styles you may notice. For your business, you may want to take one style and build it all round that. A majority of people will probably want to focus on the passive way of selling. In my life, I have noticed that there are more passive people and introverts than there are impassive people extroverts.

Now, I want to break these styles down for you and give you a better understanding of each. This is in hopes that if you choose to be a sales coach, you may be able to understand more than one style which in the end will be more profits.

Let's go backwards from the order I listed the styles in since I know there are many more passive sellers than impassive:

- **Passive**

Passive selling is pretty effective. You do not want to be labeled "pushy sales- person" and so you take this approach. As a coach, you will teach others how to get the sale without "selling to" someone. Passive selling can be achieved in a more laid back setting where people are already aware that your product or service exists.

This makes things easier for you in the long run. Passive selling may require aggressive selling at the start. This is until people are aware of your brand and company. When people become loyal customers, then they will be looking out for new products and services and special offers.

- **Aggressive**

Aggressive is when you seek after people to tell them you have a product and convince them to buy it. As I said above, when your business is new, this may be an approach you need to start with. As more people are aware of your brand, you can transition into a passive approach.

- **Consultative**

This is actually what coaching is about. As a coach, you are not just helping people understand their skills or business better, but rather acting as a type of consultant. You are the expert in your niche, so you can rest assured that there will be people who trust you for your expertise.

- **Proactive**

Proactive selling allows you to cause the sale to happen. You are not just standing to the side, then responding to the sale once a transaction occurred. The sale may never have happened if you were not proactive in it. When you are coaching people with this style, you need to emphasize the importance of being proactive. You are proactive with your sales whether you are passive or aggressive in sales.

How to implement your coaching business

Once you have read about and decided which coaching business you feel fits you best, it is time to implement it. All of these coaching businesses can begin the same way. First a good plan will need to be set in place. Follow that plan exactly how it is because consistency is important.

With your plan you should include a mind map of each component of your business. Search Google® for some sample mind maps. Here you can see all the different components and can add more or take away some as necessary. Having an illustration right before you will help you gather all the ideas possible to set your business up and run it.

Now take each section of the mind map at a time and figure out an order to put them in. There is no wrong or right order here, but your instinct may tell you to do certain things before others. Follow that instinct and refer to your resources. This may require more research to see if there is any logical order to implement your business in.

Now, take one piece at a time and execute it. Then observe what happens. The parts which work best will require less attention. Now take those pieces which did not deliver an ideal outcome. Focus on them and try to work out a way to improve it. Once it improves, keep executing it. Now repeat this now and for the life of the business.

Note that things will change as your business grows. What worked one time may not work in the future. So always be open to creating new plans for your business. Remember to also be consistent.

Resources and example coaching businesses

Resources are very important. They also help with credibility. For example, if you want to increase sales a good resource for you is a person such as Tony Robbins. Tony Robbins is a renowned leadership expert and helps people plan their businesses.

As a life coach himself, Tony has helped tons of people achieve goals the can only dream of. Part of your career as a coach is your ability to speak in front of people. Again, Tony Robbins is a great example to use. You can find out more about him by doing a quick google search.

Besides people like Tony, what other resources can you trust? If you do some more research and find peer reviewed articles, they will help tremendously. If you are not familiar with what a peer reviewed article is, they are written by experts in a particular field and reviewed by other experts in that field. After it has been carefully reviewed then it is published.

You can find peer reviewed articles, journals, and other texts of the like at your library or through the library's website. Please be advised that you should get as many resources as possible and refer back to them as needed.

Marketing your coaching business

Now that you have decided on your coaching business and have some important plans set in place, you will need to know how to market your idea and realize which ways will be most effective. No two businesses are alike, so there is no right way to market that will work every time. Even though there are people out there that say their method works, proceed with caution.

It is best to do some research and test your own methods out. Remember that you can research the internet, but get as many sources as possible. Many people will create a site or blog and say whatever they want. So when you get a good number of sites, compare the sites and blogs with the credible information you found. Take the marketing ideas that make the most sense and use them to guide you.

Marketing should also be treated similar to selling and keep in mind what I talked about in that section. As there are different selling styles, there are different sub- categories for marketing your coaching business.

For those people whom you want to do business with, these small categories are something you should really pay attention to. There are three categories, which I learnt that take some unknown out of sales and change the way you think about it from now on. One is relationship marketing, two is social marketing, and three is content marketing.

I chose these three styles because they are extremely important in a coaching business. There are other styles out there in the world but the main focus is getting some ideas across so you have a foundation to base things off of. Now let's talk about the smaller yet important sales categories.

- **Relationship Marketing**

Relationship marketing is a fairly new concept as it stands, but in reality, it is something most people learn when they get a job. What you learn is that you should treat the customer so they feel as if they are welcome in the store or company. You want them to feel at home.

This builds a relationship with the very people you want to do business with. Another way to build relationships with people is to remember things about them. When you see them face to face, try and remember their name. When they give you their information send out a birthday, holiday, or anniversary card which can help build a stronger relationship.

This is one marketing category you want to be focused on more than others. The more personable you can be, the better your business will run. Those who are experts in relationship marketing and can relay the importance of this concept can expect to have an easier time growing their coaching business.

- **Social Marketing**

This category has been around, but there are some important ground rules to adhere to. Do a bit of research on the different ways you should market through social media. It is more than just putting an affiliate like on your Facebook wall or on you Twitter feed. You have to engage the audience every way you can and NOT seem like you are just trying to get them to click a link and buy an affiliate offer.

Once you understand the ground rules, the sky is the limit with social marketing. You can join groups and go on message boards, but be warned, you want to build rapport with the members first. There are some places like the "Warrior Forum" that are designed for internet marketers. You still need to build relationships with the members before you dive right in and post your ads.

- **Content Marketing**

Content marketing has been around since the written word. People have been finding ways to communicate with other people since language began. It is something that will not soon die out, so this should be another of your focuses when it comes to marketing.

Making your business fun and engaging

Being an enthusiastic person greatly increases your ability to attract more people to your coaching business. Attracting people is way more than just speaking in an enthusiastic way and sounding exciting. You have to be authentic as well because people will be able to tell if you are or not.

If you are just going through the motions, you will not seem real or that you are really interested in what you are doing. The best way to be successful with this part is to really have an interest and passion for what you will be doing.

You also want to attract the right people to your business. Trying to get as many people as you can to jump on board and get coaching from you seems like the ideal thing, but if those people seem like they are on board then drop off the face of the planet, it will just be wasted effort in the end.

One thing I warned about early on is be careful of the resources you use. However, one thing you can do as an exercise to help your business to be more fun and engaging is to read blogs. Since many blogs are not expected to be professional and people may not be writing about the subject in the most professional manner, you can always get some good ideas from it.

When reading the blog, think about what makes reading it fun and engaging for you. Apply that to your own business and it will be easier to get motivated.

Motivation is the key to a successful coaching career.

Find out what people want and need

How do you know what people want and need? It is a great open ended question to start you out with. You will never know right off the bat, and it can be hard to pinpoint what people actually want. If you are a social person, it may be easy for you to approach someone and have a nice conversation and from there learn what they want and need.

This is considered small talk and is a great way to find the information you are looking for. On neutral ground, people are more likely to talk about superficial things. They don't know you on a personal level, so it is easier to simply talk about what is happening at the given moment. This is to your advantage. And if you are not the most social person or are shy or even a little self-conscious, don't be.

The reason being is you should not worry about what people think of you at that moment. They do not know you and if your conversation was not the greatest, they probably will not remember the negative things about it. And that is okay. Consider it practice and keep going out in the world and try again.

Once you build up confidence, you will begin to see a change in how people react to you. Take note of how things have changed and realize those changes. The more you connect with people and learn their needs, the better things will get for you.

Plan each session before you start

Hopefully you have heard of the saying, "failing to plan is planning to fail." Write this one down and put it into view either on your bathroom mirror, the bedroom or front door, or anywhere where you will see it. This will act as a reminder that you need to make sure you planned for what you will be doing from day to day.

Keep a schedule

Having a schedule is so important. You want to know when you hold coaching sessions and also know what activities you will need to do to accomplish certain goals. Many people get stuck here because structure is not a huge part of our daily lives. Get something into practice before you begin your business and make a point to follow it daily. This will be a big step toward getting into the habit of being organized and prepared.

Organization is important

Being organized and staying that way is very important. In fact this is one of the most important attributes to your business and will save you from huge headaches later. It goes along with planning as well. You plan needs to be organized and having an organized plan will help you here.

I have some tips and advice for being and staying organized and so I want you to read once, then go back and read it again. The second time you read it, you will think to yourself how you will accomplish this task. In the end I hope you will be better organized and see success down the road as a result.

Be prepared to answer questions

You want people to ask questions. That is how you know they are engaged in what you are presenting to them. You will never be able to have all the information you need set in place as to avoid any uncertainties. In fact it is actually good to have uncertainties because as you are able to answer the questions, you will also learn something new.

Coaching isn't about knowing everything, but knowing enough to help people who want it. If you do not know the answer to something, do not just tell them anything. If you do, you will be in a world of hurt in the future.

How to get your clients engaged

How do you get clients engaged? Remember earlier I said you want to attract the right type of people. So once you have the right people, then it will be that much easier for you. One thing to ask yourself is what gets you engaged? I know one thing that gets me engaged is simple; eye contact and using my name when someone speaks to me.

Acknowledge as many people as you can. "I have a bad memory", or "I'm not good with names," are the most common excuses people make. The problem is that neither excuse is accurate. You just did not "learn" how to remember someone's name. Learning and remembering go hand in hand. Find out different methods that people use to help them remember things and practice it. The best way is to try and continue to try.

Create a calendar (so people can view your schedule)

My favorite thing is to have a calendar with all my events written in. There are digital calendars you can share with people and even free software you can find from your website hosting to meet your needs for this.

Experience tells me to write everything down; EVERYTHING. If you have working experience, meaning you have held a job of some sort, you will realize that people will tell you something one time then later on, what they told you will be irrelevant. Even at your job you should write everything down not just to cover your end, but so you can refer back to it to help you remember what was said.

With the calendar software of your choice, you can have your schedule viewable to your clients and to whomever you choose. If you have workers who are helping with your business, it is a great way for them to know what is going on.

CONCLUSION

Coaching is all around you. It comes in subtle forms and other times coaching is blatantly obvious. Obviously coaching is associated with sports, but certain other life activities greatly benefit from coaching. Take the different types of coaching businesses in this article as something to compare to different life situations where coaching can be beneficial.

Remember, the most important part in starting your own coaching business is to think about and decide what it is that motivates you the most. From there, you can look at the examples above and use them as a guide as you begin to develop a plan for your business.

As the plan develops, certain strategies can be executed giving you a "jump start" for a long and successful path. Success is only measured by the results from the type of effort you put into it. It will take time and effort to start the business and keep it running. There are no easy answers and learning from others will not prevent you from making your own mistakes. It is important to make your own mistakes so you can learn from them and grow stronger.

Printed by Libri Plureos GmbH in Hamburg,
Germany

9 786069 837528